CORVETTE

The Classic American Sports Car

By David H. Jacobs

Mason Crest
450 Parkway Drive, Suite D
Broomall, PA 19008
www.masoncrest.com

© 2018 by Mason Crest, an imprint of National Highlights, Inc.

Printed and bound in the United States of America.

Series ISBN: 978-1-4222-3828-8
Hardback ISBN: 978-1-4222-3830-1
EBook ISBN: 978-1-4222-7955-7

First printing
1 3 5 7 9 8 6 4 2

Additional text by Bob Woods.

Cover photograph by NaturSports/Dreamstime.com.

Library of Congress Cataloging-in-Publication Data is on file with the publisher.

BMW

CORVETTE

FERRARI

JAGUAR

LAMBORGHINI

MERCEDES-BENZ

MUSTANG

PORSCHE

CONTENTS

KEY ICONS TO LOOK FOR

 Educational Videos: Readers can view videos by scanning our QR codes, providing them with additional educational content to supplement the text. Examples include news coverage, moments in history, speeches, iconic moments, and much more!

 Series Glossary of Key Terms: This back-of-the-book glossary contains terminology used throughout this series. Words found here increase the reader's ability to read and comprehend higher-level books and articles in this field.

 Research Projects: Readers are pointed toward areas of further inquiry connected to each chapter. Suggestions are provided for projects that encourage deeper research and analysis.

INTRODUCTION

On July 1, 1953, a birth announcement appeared in the pages of that journal of record, *The New York Times*. The small item was headlined:

SPORTS CAR PRODUCED
Chevrolet Corvette Has Body of Laminated Glass Fiber

The rest of the text, no more than a few paragraphs in all, went on to report that, a day earlier, on June 30, the first Corvette had rolled off the line at the assembly plant in Flint, Michigan. It's amusing to speculate how the average *New York Times* reader might have reacted to the news, if it was even noticed at all. The idea of an "American sports car" may well have raised a smile due to its improbability, while the body of "laminated glass fiber" (i.e., Fiberglas) might have lifted a few eyebrows.

Closer to today, on the other end of the life cycle, we have the real-life example of the late Mr. George Swanson, of Pennsylvania, who in 1994 was buried in his beloved white Corvette. Surely no pharaoh of antiquity was ever entombed with such a royal chariot. Aficionados of the car must agree that Mr. Swanson definitely had a case of Corvette Fever.

Now, with its Golden Fiftieth Anniversary only a few years away, the Corvette occupies a unique position not only in Detroit's automotive history, but also in the pantheon of American popular culture. The Corvette has been immortalized in song and story, movies and television. In this age of seen-it-all media saturation, a Corvette can still create a sensation. And, with the release of the all-new Corvette C5, it's a surety that Corvettes will go on creating a sensation well into the twenty-first century.

The smiles that once might have greeted the idea of an American sports car have long since faded away. With its high performance and bold design, the Corvette is a world-class symbol of automotive excellence. Even during the

The 1954 model continued the distinctive wire-mesh stone guards over the headlamps, part of the sports car mystique. Side trim detailing includes the chrome fin just forward of the Corvette name. Lackluster sales threatened the car's existence.

The 1964 Sting Ray coupe, now minus the controversial window divider bar. Round taillights had been a Corvette staple since 1961.

darkest days of Detroit, when the industry was awash with woes and besieged by foreign imports, Corvette never compromised those standards of superb style and technological prowess.

What other American-made car commands the loyal, and, in some cases, fanatical following of the Corvette? You don't have to be an owner to get Corvette Fever. In fact, just seeing the car may be enough to make you a believer. Just take a look at some of the beautifully photographed Corvettes in this book, and see if you don't agree. There are Corvette clubs, rallies, and events such as the annual Bloomington Gold festival in Springfield, Illinois, the nation's largest Corvette show, where hundreds of vintage 'Vettes and thousands of fans gather to celebrate the machine. The National Corvette Museum in Bowling Green, and the Corvette assembly plant across the street, are two of the most popular tourist attractions in all of their home state of Kentucky.

There's a General Motors maxim which goes, "There's a little bit of Corvette in every Chevrolet." This is almost literally true, not just for the Chevy badge but for all GM, since the Corvette has been used so often as a test bed, a proving ground, for advances in automotive technology that have eventually become industry-wide standards. The fiberglass body, disc brakes, rack-and-pinion steering, independent suspension, computerized engine control modules, and so many others, all had their initial try-outs in Corvette before being more widely adopted. And, as in the case of the revolutionary hydroformed tube rail framework in the new C5, Corvette remains at the cutting edge of technological innovation.

The history of the Corvette can be handily divided into three main phases. Phase One is its origin and development as sports car, a period stretching from 1953 through 1962. Phase Two begins with the introduction of the 1963 Sting Ray, heralding what could be called the machine's "Dream Car" phase. During this period, Corvette transcended its role as purely a sports car, and gathered a wider audience including many who were not so much sports car fans as Corvette fans. This was also the heyday of the big block engine Muscle Car Corvettes, an exciting and carefree Detroit era. The end of the Dream Car phase may be dated to the 1975 Corvette convertible, the last such roadster until its revival in 1986.

The third phase is what could be called Corvette's "Future Car" period, in which the line has weathered the climate of tough economic times, fuel shortages, and government regulations. Phase Three starts around 1976, and continues through today. As you will see, by designing their car "future-forward," Corvette has not only survived the tough times but won through to triumph, though not without many struggles.

If it's true that "there's a little bit of Corvette in every Chevy," it may also be truthfully observed that there's a little bit of the Corvette driver in every one of us.

So, fasten your seat belt, and get ready to catch the fever that needs no cure—Corvette Fever.

FOLLOWING PAGE: The first new Corvette since 1984—the 1997 C5 coupe. Highlighted by an all-aluminum LS1 5.7-liter V—8 and a revolutionary hydro-formed frame, the C5 was hailed on its debut with instant acclaim.

Marque of excellence: the distinctive "crossed flags" badge has set the seal on Chevrolet Corvettes for almost fifty years now. The flags are the Chevy banner and the checkered flag of auto racing, signifying Corvette's status as "the American sports car."

Granddaddy of them all, the original 1953 Corvette two-seater roadster, created by stylist Harley Earl and engineer Ed Cole. An eye-catching hybrid, with its unique Fiberglas body, 6-cylinder engine, and automatic transmission. All three hundred made that year were colored Polo White.

CHAPTER ONE

SPORTS CAR

The worldwide phenomenon which came to be known as "Corvette Fever" had its start about four and a half decades ago as a whim of corporate prestige. In the early 1950s, General Motors, one of Detroit's Big Three automakers, was an industrial titan in both national and international markets. The company's economic mainstay was the family car, available in a variety of makes and models, designed and built for easy, comfortable driving.

At the same time, a counter-trend was developing, numerically small at first, but a significant indicator of a change in climate. This was the sports car boomlet, begun domestically in the late 1940s by American ex-GIs, returned home after serving a European tour of duty, where they'd gotten a taste for the pure driving pleasure of low-slung, fine-tuned, high-performance sports cars, particularly British-made MGs, Triumphs, and Jaguars. These zippy foreign-made speedsters made Detroit sit up and take notice.

Accepting the Challenge

The challenge to build an American sports car was taken up, ironically, by Chevrolet, traditionally GM's most "apple pie" division. Behind the bold gamble were two extraordinary individuals, Harley Earl and Ed Cole.

Earl originally hailed from Los Angeles, where he'd been a neighbor of Hollywood's master showman of oldtime movies, Cecil B. De Mille. Earl first made a name for himself by customizing cars for silent movie film stars. He left around the same time that talkies came in, going to Detroit in 1927 to eventually become head of GM's Art and Colors Section. Earl was a master stylist (Detroitese for "designer"), the first to model cars in sculpted clay. That the Corvette has had a larger than life, theatrical presence from day one, throughout its various incarnations, is in large part due to the influence of Harley Earl.

Ed Cole was Chevrolet's Chief Engineer, tasked to turn stylists' designs into nuts-and-bolts automotive reality—a job he did so well that later he became first the head of the entire Chevrolet division, then President of GM. Earlier, in 1948, he and Earl had teamed together to create an acclaimed tail-finned Cadillac. Now, they set out to build an all-American sports car.

From a list of three hundred names, Earl finally picked the name "Corvette." In 1952, clay models were sculpted. By July of the following year, production had begun on the real thing. A key factor in the start-up was the then-revolutionary decision to make the body not of formed sheet metal, but of lightweight fiberglass. Dramatic cost savings from working in plastic not metal made the Corvette economically feasible to produce. There was some thought at the time to eventually making the switch over to metal, which was soon forgotten.

The 1953 Corvette was equipped with a modified Chevrolet Stovebolt Blue Flame L6 6-cylinder 150-horsepower engine—respectable enough, if a bit anemic for hardcharging sports car enthusiasts. An upgrade was in the works.

That first year, 1953, at the plant in Flint, Michigan, three hundred Corvettes were built. Body panel parts were manually assembled on the framework, making each car virtually hand-crafted. The combination of chassis, power-train, and body was a unique hybrid, visually striking, awkward and ungainly in other ways, the whole latent with power and possibilities.

The 1953 Corvette two-seater roadster showcased its Euro-sports car influences best in its sophisticated plastic body shell. The similarities were less evident under the hood, where the Corvette's power plant was a Blue Flame L6 6-cylinder engine, displacing 235.5 cubic inches, at 150 horsepower—respectable enough, but far from the muscular mills demanded by sports car enthusiasts. It was available only in Powerglide automatic transmission, again not much of a thrill for the speedster set, although the shift was installed on the floor to counterfeit the look of a manual gearshift.

More evidence of its rugged sports car ethos was the lack of the amenities, such as exterior door handles and roll-up windows (glass side curtains were supplied instead). It was a convertible only, no hardtop. The suspension was bad, the ride rough.

And yet, there was something about the Corvette, some indefinable sense of dash or élan that clicked with the automotive public, intriguing them. A handsome beast, with its toothy front grille and rocketship taillights, its

The driver needed a mighty wide angle of vision to monitor the widespread instrument panel of the 1953 Corvette. At the center of the display is the tachometer. All model interiors were white and red.

ody Polo White with a Sportsman Red interior, it was a hit of that year's GM Futurama auto show.

On January 1,1954, production facilities were switched over to the St. Louis Assembly Plant. The Corvette was now available in four different colors. It came with courtesy lights, windshield washers, and directional signals. The red-topped, red-trimmed white instrument panel featured a wide-angle gauge display centered around the tachometer.

Sales were not great. Corvette was slipping. At this point entered the third member of the triumvirate responsible for nursing the infant machine past its birth pangs. Style studio head Earl and Chevrolet's Chief Engineer Cole were now joined by motor maestro Zora Arkus-Duntov. Russian-born and Belgian-raised, Duntov was an engineer and auto racer who'd done important work with superchargers in Europe between the wars, later emigrating to the United States. He liked this new Corvette, with its stylish body and untapped potential. He wrote a letter to Cole, saying so. He was an outsider, a walk-in, Cole wound up making him project engineer, that is, Corvette's Chief Engineer, a position held by Duntov until his retirement some twenty years later.

The team was in place. Earl, Cole, Duntov—Corvette's Big Three. The first move was to drop a 265-cubic inch, overhead V-8 engine into the front of the 1955 roadster. Equipped with a single four-barrel Carter carburetor, it could generate 195 horsepower, finally giving sports car fans some real muscle under the hood.

It helped, but was it enough? The crunch was coming, the showdown to determine whether the car would live or die.

The 1953 Corvette's rear styling treatment was distinguished by rocketship tail-light pods, dual exhaust pipes, and an elegantly abbreviated chrome bumper strip. There was also a trunk, an item which would be far from standard equipment in the future.

The Model-Saver

In its struggle for survival, Corvette's unlikeliest ally was its arch rival and pretender to the throne of American two-seater king, the Ford Thunderbird. Launched in 1954, Thunderbird was aimed at the same market as Corvette. Worse, it was getting it. In 1955, there were sixteen thousand Thunderbirds sold compared to less than five thousand Corvettes.

In business, when something isn't working, there's always a tendency to say, *let's cut our losses and walk away*, a tendency which increases as one gets farther away from those whose baby is on the chopping block. Some upper management factions at GM were for killing the Corvette. What stymied the cancellation was the fear that it would leave the market wide open for the T-Bird.

It's what you don't see on this 1955 Corvette that's the key factor; namely, the 265-cid, 195-horsepower overhead V-8 engine under the hood. 4,700 Corvettes were sold that year.

'56 and '57

The 1956 Corvette was allowed to go into production, but the message from up-stairs was clear: *This better be good, it's make or break time.*

Corvette's first restyling marked a significant upgrade. A makeover model, it was one sharp car. The 1956 Corvette was available as a convertible and, for the first time, as a coupe, courtesy of a removable hardtop option. Standard was a 265-cubic inch V-8 engine with 225 horsepower. Also standard was the new three-speed manual transmission with floorshift, nudging Powerglide automatic transmission into the options list.

The design possibilities inherent in the original model were now brought to fruition by Earl. Perhaps the most striking element was the treatment of the concave bodyside coves, a distinctive touch that became a signature motif until the next generation of Corvettes in 1963. The coves were set off by neat chrome trim and further stylized by a duo-tone color contrast with the rest of the car body.

The 1956 Corvette was a make-over model from the Earl/Cole team, with the assistance of racer-engineer Duntov. It had a 225-horse-power V-8 engine and manual transmission. Perhaps not so coincidentally, that same year safety belts were first offered as an option.

The 1956 Corvette SK-2 was a unique concept car designed by stylist Harley Earl for his son, Jerry. Its sleek styling and muscular contours foreshadowed future generations of Corvettes yet to come. Legend has it that Earl designed the original Corvette to keep his son out of European sports cars.

This 1957 Corvette displays bezel-mounted headlamps, introduced during the previous year's makeover, replacing the earlier wire-screened lamps. On the hood badge, the V-shaped symbol below the crossed flags denotes a V-8 engine. As in all models since the original, the rearview mirror is mounted on top of the dash.

The headlamps were redone, eliminating the inset lights with their protective wire mesh stone guards. Rear twin pod rocketship taillights were out, replaced by semi-frenched taillights whose lenses conformed to the curved rear fenders. Attention was paid to the niceties, as seen in the addition of roll-up windows and outside push-button door handles. There was a three-spoked racing-style steering wheel.

A purely decorative touch was given by the twin simulated front fender air scoops, whose only function was to look good. The hood ornament displayed the badge's crossed flags above a stylized V-shape (as in V-8).

The promotional slogan blazoned on the advertising for the 1956 Corvette proclaimed, "Action is the Keynote!" The machine lived up to its billing in more ways than one, clicking both with car buyers and the powers that be at GM.

It's no exaggeration to say that this was the model that saved the line. The corner had been turned, leaving a clear road ahead.

The 1957 Corvette's slogan was "Drive for Power." Powering that drive was a new standard 283-cubic inch V-8 engine with 220 horsepower. Optional fuel injection systems that did away with the carburetor to deliver fuel directly to the cylinders were now available, thus inaugurating the era of fuel-injected "fuelie" Corvettes (1957–65).

One fuel-injected option goosed the engine from a standard 220 up to 250 horsepower. A critical boundary was crossed by the Ramjet fuel injector option whose 283-cubic inch engine cranked out 283 horsepower, thus establishing a one-to-one parity between cid/hp. Also boosting the engine's performance was a high (10:1) compression ratio, and a special camshaft, valve springs, and lifters—all this on a small block engine.

Also sustaining the drive to power was a new four-speed manual gearbox. All non-standard engine packages were identified by side crossed flag emblems, and the words "Fuel Injection" on the rear.

Ironically, the rival car whose presumed market share threat to the Corvette had kept the latter alive during its crisis, was itself given the ax, as the Ford Thunderbird was canceled in 1957.

1957 saw the launch of the fuel-injected Corvette. The "Fuelie" package boosted the 283-cid, 220-horsepower standard engine up to 283-horsepower, setting up a one-to-one equivalence between cid and horsepower.

Design studio concept cars blaze the trail for standard production models that follow. This 1958 Corvette Special foreshadows the 1961 Mako Shark 1, which was integral to the development of the Sting Ray.

Anticipating the Batmobile, this 1958 Lister Corvette show car features dynamic curvilinear body design, side rail exhaust pipes, and an all-important 327-cid engine.

orward into Style

958 found the Corvette at midcourse of its first phase. That year's model oasted a bundle of new options and styling touches. There were four different engine packages and three transmission options. The topline engine package unched 315 horsepower from its 283-cubic inch V-8.

The 1958 Corvette was the bulkiest and most ornate yet. Most dramatic of ts stylistics were the new quad headlamps, each twin set divided by chrome ender trim strips. Also dramatic, though nonfunctional, were the dummy ir scoops at the corners of the massive front bumper—visually dynamic but trictly decorative. Where the snouty front grille once had thirteen teeth eleven long ones and two shorties at the corners), it now had nine. The hood vas adorned with dummy washboard louvers. The rear decklid sported twin hrome strips. Whitewall tires were optional.

The hardtop's Plexiglas windows tended to scratch. A new dashboard layout eatured a center console for better instrument display. The speedometer now opped out at 160 miles per hour, up 20 miles from the previous version. The achometer topped out at 6,000 revolutions per minute, although the hottest engine package could reach 8,000 rpms. Handling was improved by a new rear nti-sway bar.

1958 saw the retirement of Art and Color Studio chief Harley Earl. The post of orvette's head stylist would be filled by Bill Mitchell, who would later become iM's Vice President of Design, continuing to dictate Corvette styling through-ut his tenure, until his retirement in 1977.

1958's Corvette took a swerve toward Grand Touring/GT car country. This fuel-injected model features new quad headlamps, a redesigned grille, and dummy front air scoops. Top engine option had an output of 315-horsepower.

Building early
Corvettes

1959 was almost as important for its deletions as its additions. Gone were some of last year's stylistic "bells and whistles," the dummy washboard louvers and chrome decklid strips. The subtle refinements helped to point the Corvette back to its original sports car design ethos. The car was beginning to attract notice on the national and international racing circuit.

Dual-spinner wheel covers were now slotted to increase cooling air flow to the brakes. The tachometer now top-lined at 7,000 rpms. Bucket seats were upholstered in vinyl over sponge rubber, color-coordinated, of course. Recessed dummy vents were added, their fender panels decorated with the crossed flags emblem. Minus the dummy louvers, the hood's twin ridged windsplits accented the car's forward visual thrust. This car looked fast even when it was sitting still.

"Designed for Personal Sports Car Comfort" was 1960's slogan, as that year's model saw steady incremental improvements. Corvette was available in convertible and coupe, with convertibles outselling coupes as they had from the start, and would continue to do so until 1969. The 1960 Corvette had five engine option packages, the beefiest of which could put out 315 horsepower. There were three different ear-axle ratio options, including Positraction slip differential, and three transmission options.

1960 also had a couple of noticeable lasts. It was the last year for the stylized V-shape/crossed flags hood emblem, and the last year for the sloping rear deck with protective wraparound bumper.

The chrome on the 1959 Corvette was cut back from the previous year's, but was still pretty heavy, as can be seen here. Twin dummy front air scoops offset the weighty bumper and grille assemblage.

By 1959, most of the chrome stripping was gone, though the quad-lights fender trim remains. The leaner and meaner Corvette hearkened back to the model's high-performance roots. 230-horsepower was standard.

The crossed flags emblem decorates the fender panels forward of the duo-tone bodyside coves on this 1959 model. Thin chrome trim accents the design. The slotted dual-spinner wheel covers funnel a cooling air flow to the brakes.

Lasts and Firsts

1961–62 marked the final flowering of Corvette's first phase, a transition time of notable lasts and firsts.

The 1961 Corvette was billed as a "New Look" car. Its forerunner was a Sting-ray racer which had been built from a 1957 Corvette by Bill Mitchell in the late 1950s. The 1961 model would bear his hallmark. Key to the design was the rear body treatment, with the tapered "ducktail" rear deck, for a jaunty, stream-lined look. Another first were the round taillight lenses, a clean and elegant styling touch.

The toothy grille was out, replaced by a more modernistic rectangular mesh grille. Front fender crossed-flags were out, replaced by three-bar trim. The Cor-vette name and crossed flags, minus a badge emblem, decorated the hood.

It was also the last of the 283-cubic inch engine. 1961 saw the advent of XP-755 Mako Shark I, a GM show car designed by Larry Shinoda—a shape of things to come that would take form in the Sting Ray just beyond the horizon ...

FOLLOWING PAGE:
The 1961 model had a new look. Gone was the toothy grille, replaced by a more subtle mesh grille. The crossed flags hood emblem appears over the Cor-vette name minus its framing badge insig-nia. Also new is the rear "ducktail" styling.

The 1961 model eliminated the tradition-al sloping rear deck with wraparound bumper to achieve its signature ducktail style. By 1962, the bodyside coves had also been downsized.

Rear detailing of a 1959 Corvette high-lights the Euro-style treatment of the tail-lights, with the lens integrated into the overall body curve. Similarly, the tailpipe conforms to the rear bumper pod.

1959 saw the increasing use of tough, light-weight aluminum components in the Corvette's 283-cid V-8 engine, upping performance specs. There was big muscle in that small-block mill.

The rectangular mesh grille on the red 1962 roadster displays that year's anodized blacked-out grille style. 1962 Corvettes would see the last of exposed headlights and solid axles.

The interior of the 1961 Corvette. The cockpit had been redesigned in 1959, regrouping the instrument display in a more driver-friendly cluster. The "Wonderbar" radio is set vertically in the central console.

1962 was the valedictory year for the first wave Corvettes, but the mood was confident, forward-looking. Paving the way for next generation was the replacement of the 283-cid engine by a new standard 327-cubic inch V-8, destined to become Detroit's popular V-8 ever. The small block engine delivered a standard 250 horsepower, a twenty percent increase over the previous year's mill. The 1962 fuel-injected Sebring Corvette 327 engine package could reach 360 horsepower.

1962's car showed an anodized black-out grille and smaller bodyside coves. Whitewalls were narrower. New rocker panel trim made the low-slung craft seem even closer to street-level. Chrome stripping no longer outlined the body coves.

This was the last year for Corvette's exposed quad headlamps and front fender chrome trim strips, the last year of solid axles. It was also the last year that Corvettes had trunks, until their reappearance in the 1997 C5.

The 1962 roadster boasted its first-ever 327-cid small block V-8 engine, with 250-horsepower standard, an instant Detroit classic. It was also the last Corvette to have a trunk until the 1997 C5.

*The American Dream—the 1963 Chevrolet Corvette Sting
Ray Coupe, to give it its official title. Of course, it was also
available as a convertible. Either way, a revolutionary
body shell was mounted on a 327-cid engine and chassis
unchanged from 1962's high-performance standards.*

CHAPTER TWO

DREAM CAR

The distinctive front-hinged, forward-opening clamshell hood opens on the classic 327-cid small block V-8 engine in a 1963 Corvette. The 327-mill ranks as Detroit's all-time most popular small block.

Sports car morphed into dream car. That's what happened when the 1963 Corvette Sting Ray was introduced. The model delivered sports car quality and high performance, while in many ways approaching a grand touring car. Particularly in the later years, during the heyday of the big block era, a Corvette could be fully loaded with a package of weighty and expensive luxury options, including AM-FM radio, power steering and windows, and air conditioning, and still remain a formidable speed machine. That kind of muscle had its price—in low mileage and high auto emissions, which would eventually doom the big block behemoths.

There were no engine changes in the 1963 Corvette, but something new was going on under its unique bodyshell. To the car's steel ladder frame were added a steel Bird Cage framework, providing reinforced support beneath the plastic. The Bird Cage framework would remain integral to the line for the next thirty-plus years.

The Corvette Sting Ray Coupe, as it was officially titled, was a true grand touring car. The design was radical, its most unusual element the vertical splitter bar bisecting the fastback rear window. It was controversial even during in-house production, with Bill Mitchell arguing that the splitter was the heart and soul of the design, while engineer Duntov rightly pointed out that the bar created a hazardous driving blind spot. Mitchell won the point, the coupe went out with splitter bar intact.

The existence of the blind spot caused many owners to convert to a splitter-free rear window job, making the original split-window 1963 coupe the rarest of all Corvettes. So rare, that in later years some owners tried to convert their modified uni-window fastbacks back to their original divider mode.

The splitter was one distinct element in a pacesetting design. A slope hood dipped beneath the fenderlines, its forward thrust heightened by a centerline windsplit arrow. Its lines were unmarred thanks to a set of concealed rotating headlamps. A pair of muscular front fender bulges had an organic quality suggestive of the seagoing manta ray that was the car's namesake.

1963 Corvettes had wider wheel rims, though the custom wire-spoke job shown here was not standard issue. More important was the Sting Ray's new four-wheel independent suspension.

A rear view of the 1963 coupe showcases the controversial split window with structural rail "stinger." Unaltered originals are few and costly, making this the most collectible Corvette.

The seeds of 1956's experimental SK-2 came to fruition in the 1963 Corvette Grand Sport special edition. With wraparound windshields a thing of the past, all Sting Rays now had front side ventipanes.

The wraparound curved windshield which had been such a strikingly successful feature in the previous generation was out. The new windshield was fastened to side window posts, while the windows had front side ventipanes.

Earlier models had front-wheel suspension, but the 1963 edition offered complete four-wheel independent suspension, the rear suspension was now a three-link independent setup with a single transverse leaf spring.

There were wider wheel rims, and an adjustable steering column. Options included a variety of drivetrains, power steering, power brakes, and a leather-upholstered interior.

A newly redesigned three-spoke steering wheel afforded a clear, unimpeded view of the instrument panel. The sleekly restyled cockpit made the most of its limited space by placing the AM-FM radio vertically in the center console. The standard tachometer was set to redline at 5,000 rpms. A new crossed flags emblem blazoned the hood, with a badge medallion at the rear, below the splitter. Taillights were twinned at the upper corners of the rear panel and dual exhaust pipes emerged from within concentric circle housings.

The year 1964 delivered the verdict on the Corvette's fastback splitter bar. It was gone, never to return. Side louvers allowed greater ventilation for an essentially unchanged engine, though the fuel-injected 327 small block could reach 375 horsepower. The muffler was improved, while new springs afforded a smoother, more quiet ride.

The model made some moves in the direction of a luxury car. There were new wheel covers, and new rocker panels provided solid visual undergirding. Inside, for the true devotee of luxury, there was a walnut-finish steering wheel rim, and a chrome gear knob shift—not bad for a price tag under five thousand dollars (at 1964 rates of exchange).

Beyond lay the dawn of the big block engine Corvette.

The 1964 coupe with optional side rail exhaust. The standard model featured chrome rocker panels and a new walnut-finish steering wheel rim, a nod to GT car luxury.

The 1964 Sting Ray with a fuel-injected 327 small block engine had an output of 375-horsepower (standard was 250 horses). That year's model also boasted an improved ride and muffler.

The 1965 Corvette introduced a new four-wheel disc braking system and independent rear suspension. The grille and rocker panels were subtly restyled. The base price was around $5,000.

The 1965 Sting Ray convertible displays the crossed flags logo at the point of the hood's aerodynamic windsplit. The newly redesigned emblem first bowed in 1963.

Big

It might have been the ultimate small block engine, the 1965 Corvette Ramjet fuel-injected 327-cubic inch V-8, capable of 375 horsepower. But it was the last of its breed. This was the final year of the Corvette fuelie, the same year which saw the debut of its successor.

This was the Turbo-Jet 396-cubic inch L78 V-8, the first of the line's big block engines, with an output of 425 horsepower—the progenitor of the Detroit Muscle Car, free (at least temporarily) from regulatory constraints. Massive motors powered the short-lived but intense era of mega-muscle machines.

The 1965 Corvette was newly equipped with a four-wheel disc brake system, timed perhaps not so coincidentally to coincide with the arrival of the big block engines. An outside exhaust pipe was an option. The front grille was restyled for more rectangularity. There were no depressions or trim on the hood. Smooth-finish rocker panels were new. The interior showed a twin-cowl dashboard. The roof had a centerline windsplit, and the 396 edition had a unique and distinctive windsplit arrow.

The power bulge on the hood and the side exhaust rails identify this 1966 Sting Ray coupe as the bearer of a 427-cid big block Mark IV engine, with 425-horsepower. It could go from zero to sixty in 5.7 seconds. A classic muscle car.

The L-88 racing package option was introduced in 1967. The aluminum-headed 427-Mark IV engine's output ranged from an impressive 430 horsepower all the way up to an astounding 600-hp. The hood design was unique to that year.

"A True All-American Sports Car," was that year's slogan. 1965 also saw the exhibition of the Mako Shark II showcar, which would prefigure the 1968 second generation Sting Ray.

The 1966 Corvette's small block 327 gave a standard 300 horsepower, with various options tweaking it to 350-hp. The fastgrowing cult of big block enthusiasts could opt for the hulking 427-cubic inch V-8 engine with 425 horsepower, capable of going from zero to sixty in 5.7 seconds. Boosting the 427 engine was a bigger bore, longer stroke, bigger valves, and a high-lift camshaft. It needed the cooling provided with two sets of three front side vents. It could be identified by the funnel-shaped power bulge on the hood. All models were equipped with new three-spoke wheel covers.

Unique to the 1967 Corvette was a new hood design featuring a large, forward-facing air scoop over the windsplit arrow. The 427 edition is further distinguished by a striped, two-tone version of the design.

Extra engine-cooling ability was provided by additional front side vents. It was needed by mills like the new racing package option L88 427-cubic inch Mark IV engine, with 430 horsepower. 430 was the standard rating, but the aluminum-headed engine could be customized all the way up to an awesome 500 horsepower.

While the model was bulking up its powerplant, it was also making luxury moves. There was a safety-padded dash. Cast-aluminum wheels were optional, as was a rear deck luggage rack, and even a ski rack.

The 1967 muscle car Sting Ray with a 427-Mark IV engine can be identified by the large, forward-facing air scoop over the hood windsplit arrow.

Stingray, Too

What's in a name? From its inception back in 1963, through to 1967, the car was the "Sting Ray." From 1969 on, the car was the "Stingray." But in 1968, the year of the launching of the second generation Sting Ray/Stingray, the cars themselves were nameless, bare of any identifying model name tags. By any name, though, the 1968 Corvette, with its wild design and muscular engine options, was the closest the average driver would ever come to getting behind the wheel of a real live Batmobile. Any driver of this Corvette couldn't be blamed for feeling a little bit above average.

The Sting Ray restyle was overseen by Dave Holls, who had designed the earlier Mako Shark II showcar. The model built on the Sting Ray's existing engine and chassis (the wheelbase remained the same 98 inches it had been since 1963). The bodyshell design featured a nipped-in waist and long, flowing curves for a look of speed and power. The shape was dubbed the "Coke bottle" design, due to its fancied resemblance to the then-current curvilinear Coca Cola glass bottles. Working with a plastic bodyshell made the design do-able and affordable, unlike working in a medium such as sheet metal which, even if it could have been shaped into those complex curves, would have proved prohibitively expensive to do so.

Another bold stylistic stroke was the sculptural treatment of the cutaway fastback, where twin roof flanges swept back in sharp curves to merge imperceptibly with the rear deck lid, forming an arched canopy over the rear window. Front and rear lip spoilers added ripples of power.

The basic design was so successful that, except for changes made to meet federally mandated bumper safety standards, the body remained essentially unchanged through to 1982 and the next generation of C4 Corvettes.

FOLLOWING PAGE: Sleek beauties like this 1974 roadster remained bestsellers despite the fuel crisis. But the 350-cid standard engine continued on a downward trend of diminished horsepower.

There was something new and wondrous under the sun with the launch of the 1963 Corvette Sting Ray, its signature nameplate proudly proclaiming the advent of an all-American dream machine.

A stellar lineup of Sting Rays, one from each of the years from 1963–67, with a 1967 L-88 occupying the lead-off position.

1968 marked the second coming of the Corvette Ray. Just as the 1963 Sting Ray had been built on the previous year's engine and chassis, so, too, did the 1968 Corvette build on a pre-existing platform. The standard 327-small block delivered 350-horsepower.

The 1968 model came equipped with a standard 327-cubic inch engine with base 300 horsepower. Six engine options were available, including a 350-horsepower Turbo-Fire, and big block 427s in L71, L88, and L89 versions. A chilling reminder of muscle car mortality came that year when the Corvette engines were fitted with Air Injection Reactors, the first auto emissions controls ...

The car was fitted with a new twenty-gallon plastic fuel tank. The concealed rotating headlamps of the previous Sting Ray were replaced by new pop-up headlamps, and there were pop-up windshield wipers, too. The engine was cooled by two sets of four front side fender vents.

The coupe had a T-top roof with removable panels. In the automatic transmission option, Powerglide had been replaced by Turbo Hydra-Matic.

Front and rear chrome bumpers were thin, almost minimal. The front bumper framed a narrow horizontal blacked-out wire mesh grille. On the rear panel between the taillights was the neatly lettered legend: "Corvette."

The 1968 Corvette was a controversial model in Detroit circles, including the automotive press, some of whom critiqued the design as owing too much to the psychedelic spirit of the moment. But it was unquestionably popular with the car-buying public, while current opinion rightly holds the car to be a classic of freewheeling Detroit design.

The Car With No Name: the 1968 Corvette has a blank space over the front fender louvers where its name should appear. This was the "Coke bottle" design, so-called because its nipped-in waist and flaring curves evoked the shape of the popular soft drink's bottle.

The 1968 Corvette had a blank space above the front fender louvers, where the name should have gone. In 1969, that space was filled, with the word "Stingray" written in cursive chrome script. The year before, the car had gotten a startlingly new body design. This year, it got a new engine.

The small block 327-cubic inch engine was out, replaced by a 350-cubic inch small block capable of a top output of 350 horsepower. The big block option, a 427-cubic inch mill, could reach 430 horsepower. (Worth noting for the historical record is the rare, exotic 1969 Corvette ZL-1 coupe, whose all-aluminum 427-cubic inch engine was one of the most muscular packages ever offered to the public. Only two were installed and sold, but the ZL-1 was, indeed, a regular production option.)

Responding perhaps to criticism that the previous year's instrument panel was too crowded and busy, this year's model had a newly arranged instrument cluster at the upper center console. The tachometer toplined at 7,000 rpms.

A new option for 1969 was a built-in security car alarm system. Security concerns figured largely in the coupe, finally surpassing the convertible in sales that year, for the first time in Corvette history.

A milestone was reached on November 19, 1969, at the St. Louis assembly plant, as a gold convertible rolled off the line. It was Corvette's two hundred and fifty thousandth car, marking the production of a quarter million machines.

1969 saw the official changeover from Sting Ray to Stingray. This muscular beast is a 427 L-88 options package that could generate 435-horsepower. Six different engine options were available.

1969 Corvettes replace the standard 327-small block engine with a 350-cid overhead V-8 small block with 350-horsepower

The Stingray was essentially unchanged from 1968 to 1972, but there were some subtle stylistic modifica-tions. This 1971 coupe displays the "egg-crate" front grille with matching side fender grilles, which first debuted in 1970.

The 1970 Corvette LTl's 350-cid small black had 370-horsepower. The package can be identified by the special hood design with the visor shaped rear-facing scoop.

Twilight Time

The 1970–72 Corvette coupes and convertibles are all very much of a piece, basically sharing the same Stingray platform with minimal body alterations. Much of what was new was beneath the hood. A 1970 option was the small block LT1 350-cubic inch engine with solid lifters, with a top rate of 370 horsepower. LT1s had a special visor-shaped rear-facing hood scoop.

Biggest of the big blocks was the 454-cubic inch Mark IV V-8 engine, potentially able to top out at 465 horsepower, but in reality suppressed by pollution control devices to a still impressive 425 horsepower. The 1970 Clean Air Act became law, ensuring further stifling of the big block breed.

The 1970 Corvette had a restyled eggcrate grille, with the grille pattern repeated on the front side fender vent areas. Above the vents appeared the cursive script "Stingray" name. The smooth-faced rocker panels had new angled lines and there was a square-shaped exhaust pipe. In the cockpit, the motif of deeply recessed instruments continued.

In 1971, all Corvettes were made to run on unleaded fuel. Otherwise, the 1971 and 1972 models were virtually unchanged. During this period of the early 1970s, Corvette's Chief Engineer Duntov crusaded to build a mid-engine Corvette, with the engine seated in a transverse mounting. Freed from the necessity of placing the engine in front, the stylists would be able to reach new heights of streamlined body design. Ultimately the mid-engine was vetoed, the thinking being that it would be a too-radical departure from the Corvette line of development and alienate owners. The turndown was a great frustration to Duntov, who would retire in 1974, though remaining active in Corvette activities and events for more than two decades after, until his death in 1996.

The 1972 model year saw the last of the chrome-bumpered Corvettes. The next year, the chrome front bumper was gone, replaced by a federally

Shadows fall on this 1972 coupe, last of the line to bear a chrome front bumper, due to federally mandated safety regulations. Just up the road lay an uncertain new climate of fuel shortages and industry turmoil.

mandated low-impact crash resistant plastic bumper. Stylistically, the new bumper was skillfully integrated into the car's lines, anchoring and accenti[n]g the long sweeping slope of the hood. The bumper also served as an eye-plea[s]ing frame for the grille. On the hood was a crossed-flags badge medallion. The grille itself had been redone with a more subdued treatment, while the grille pattern on the front side louvers were gone.

In 1973, a built-in anti-theft alarm system became standard Corvette equip[ment]. Here was a car worth stealing, in coupe or convertible.

In 1974, the rear bumper got the same safety makeover that the front had gotten the year before, and again, the end result smoothly meshed with the car's stylish curves.

Convertibles had outsold coupes for most of Corvette's history, but this 1974 roadster was an endangered species. After 1975, it would go on hiatus until 1986. 1974 saw the last of the big block muscle car engine option packages.

This was the quiet, conservative 1973 coupe owned by a little old lady who only took it out for a drive once every Sunday. Well, maybe not. That was the year that anti-theft devices became standard Corvette equipment.

More importantly, the year marked the end of big block Corvettes. Air quality standards, oil embargoes, long lines at the fuel pumps—the world had shrunk, becoming too small for the muscle cars. It was the last hurrah of the big block 454s. The 1975 Corvettes came only with the small block 327, still an engine with plenty of zing.

Another gloomy milestone was reached in 1975, with the passing of the Corvette convertible. Security concerns and, of greater concern, impending anti-rollover legislation prompted the corporate decision to kill the roadster after this year, ending a tradition that stretched back to the car's creation.

But the convertible would return (in 1986), and as for Corvette, why, it never went away.

The 1973 coupe with a removable T-top Targa roof. The square-shaped exhaust pipes were first introduced in 1970. In 1974, the rear bumper would undergo its own federal safety standard makeover.

1973's new low-impact bumper was skillfully integrated by Corvette's stylists and engineers into the overall body design. But imagine the reaction of the driver who saw this custom coupe coming up fast in his rearview mirror.

*Custom style shops offered Corvette owners
even further high-performance refinements, as
in this 1977 Sebring Greenwood conversion. It's
all part of this thing called "Corvette Fever."*

CHAPTER THREE

FUTURE CAR

The global fuel crunch in the mid-1970s ushered in a decade and more of hard times for Detroit, with the Big Three being besieged by quality control problems and fast-selling foreign imports. Corvette remained relatively immune to these shocks, perhaps because as a prestige, high-performance line—as the American sports car—its reputation for quality remained outstanding. More, the Corvette had transcended its category to become an institution. Moving beyond its sports car origins, it had attracted a wider following of owners who were not necessarily sports car fans, but who were Corvette fans. It's an intense feeling that goes beyond brand loyalty to become part of Corvette Fever.

From 1975 through to the end of the decade, there was a sense that Corvette was marking time. Standards were maintained, it was a quality product, but it was little changed from the original Stingray II platform. Which meant at the least that it was a great-looking hot car. Much of the interest in the period is supplied by silver anniversary special editions.

1978 marked Corvette's twenty-fifth year. Technically, all of that year's cars were 25th Anniversary editions, with a fastback decorated with a Silver Anniversary commemorative badge replacing the crossed flags emblem. The fastback featured an oversized wraparound backlight-window. An engine option was the L82 350-cubic inch V-8.

That same year, a Corvette took its first turn as the official pace car of the Indianapolis 500 auto race, a welcome chore it would undertake again in 1986 and 1995. To honor the

The 1976 coupe embodies the Sting Ray in its vigorous midyears. The basic 1968 model platform was carried through with minimal changes until 1982, when the next generation was launched.

Jay Leno and the Stingray

The 1976 coupe with optional L-82 package with a 350-cid engine, knocked down by emission controls and lower compression ratios to about 205-horsepower. A 327-engine was standard.

occasion, Corvette issued a 62nd Indy 500 Pace Car Replica. This special edition had a 350-cubic inch, 220 horsepower engine. It had a black upper body and a silver metallic lower body, front and rear spoilers, alloy wheels, and wide Goodyear tires. Goodyear established an association with Corvette which has continued through to today's C5.

An even more striking special edition was the 1978 B2Z Corvette, with its unique two-tone silver paint job, the upper body silver metallic, the lower body charcoal silver. It had aluminum wheels and dual sports mirrors.

The 1979 model offered an L48 350-cubic inch engine with added horse-power. 1980 marked an interim restyling, as Dave McLellan, Corvette's Chief Engineer since 1975, made the first significant modifications in the car since 1968. The years between had seen foreign imports make significant inroads into the American car market, and the lessons of that were reflected in Corvette's 1980 makeover.

The key concepts were fuel efficiency, high technology, and aerodynamics The 1980 model was cut, trimmed, and restyled to shed some 250 pounds. There was a front air dam and streamlined low-profile hood, black louvers over the fender vents, and a rear bumper cover with integral spoiler.

1978 was Corvette's Twenty-Fifth Anniversary, and all editions of that year's model had a special Silver Anniversary badge, as well as a fastback and a wraparound backlight. And to think that some skeptics in 1953 said it'd never last!

A 1978 Indianapolis 500 Pace Car replica, commemorating Corvette's role in that year's running of the sixty-second edition of the auto racing classic. An optional 350-engine package could do 220-horsepower, as the horses began to climb yet again.

The 1980 Corvette's bodyshell was cut and trimmed along more Euro-style aerodynamic styling parameters, with a lower profile and greater fuel efficiency.

The 1980 coupe—with front air dam, low-profile roof, black louvered fender vents, and a rear bumper cover with integral spoiler to keep from going airborne.

Due to federal regulations, the speedometer toplined at a mere 85 miles per hour. Undaunted Corvette owners used the tachometer for a more accurate reading of what was going on under the hood.

In 1981, Corvette moved its production center from St. Louis, Missouri, to the new high-tech facility at Bowling Green, Kentucky. That year's Corvette incorporated cybernetics into the platform via the Computer Command Control emissions system. The model also offered an optional see-through T-top roof.

1982 said farewell to the last of the Old Guard Stingrays, sending them off with a Crossfire fuel-injected 5.7-liter-V-8 engine option. The L83 200-horse-power V-8 was standard. There was also a special Collector's Edition with a lifting glass hatchback.

The Stingray II platform had thrived for fifteen years, and for most of that time had been a cutting-edge car.

1979 was the last year for the Stingray's classic profile and free-flowing bodyshell muscularity, while the L-48 engine option continued the trend of increased horsepower.

Stealth Car

C-4 is a type of plastic explosive. C4, the next generation Corvette, also had an explosive impact, becoming the most successful model in the line's history. C4 was the designation of the platform, the basic car, namely the powertrain, chassis, and dimensional specifications. The driving environment and the wants and needs of the buyers had changed radically since the days of the car' origins in the early 1950s. C4 used high technology and aero-efficiency to adap to changing times.

The project was born at the GM Technical Center in Warren, Michigan. It had begun in 1978, under the stewardship of Chief Engineer Dave McLellan an Chevy 3 Style Studio head Jerry Palmer. With the project nearing completion, there were no 1983 Corvettes. Instead, the 1982 model continued in production, while the line at the assembly plant in Bowling Green was retooled and rege-ared to make the all-new 1984 C4 Corvette.

The designers labored to reduce the coefficient of drag, the formula-derived number which expressed the vehicle's aerodynamic efficiency. The lower the

The 1987 roadster's aero-efficient bodyshell covered a new uniframe chassis. The 1986 edition was an Indy 500 Pace Car and winner of Motor Trend's *Car of the Year award (as was the 1984 coupe).*

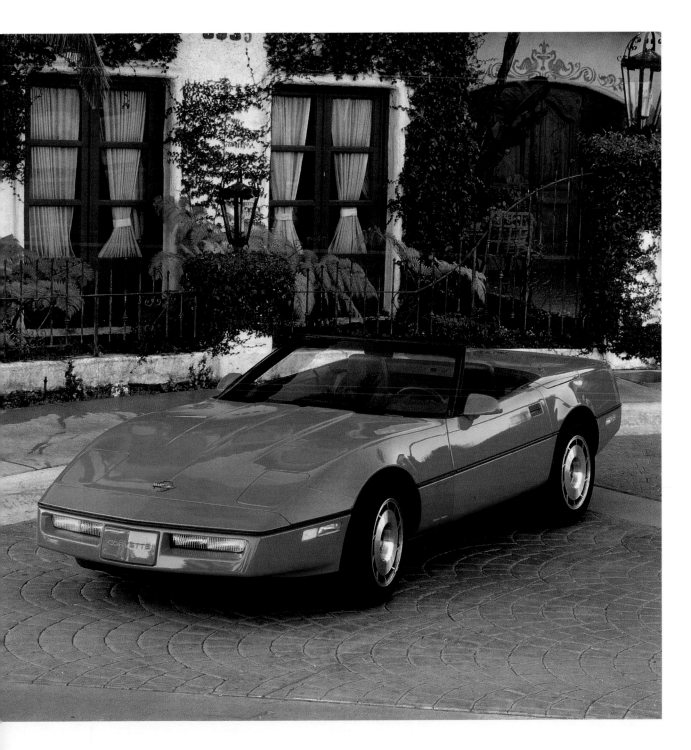

The successor to the Stingray was the all-new Corvette C4 coupe,
which debuted in 1984 to become the most successful line in the
history of the model. In 1986, the C4 roadster was unveiled, the
first convertible since 1975. Shown here is a 1987 model.

number, the more streamlined and efficient the car, since drag increases air resistance, negatively impacting on speed, mileage, and performance. Corvette was in the realm of Stealth technology, similar to that used in radar-evasive aviation, to minimize the forward profile.

With its rounded corners and elegant geometric lines, the 1984 Corvette showed the influence of the leading Euro-stylists, although the long sloping hood was pure signature Corvette. The car was over thirty percent more

erodynamically efficient than the previous model. The fastback window's wooping curve energized a wider, blockier rear. Wider tires helped accent the tail's chunky solidity.

Beneath the plastic shell, there was a uniframe chassis and Bird Cage-style steel supports. It was powered by an L83 Crossfire 5.7-liter V-8 engine, with 205 horsepower. The hinged clamshell hood was forward-opening. There was rack-and-pinion steering and disc brakes. In a nod to the computer age, the

The 1987 Corvette C4 coupe had a standard L-83 5.7-liter V-8 engine with tuned port injection, as high technology computer chips and sensors became integral to the total automotive package.

instruments had digital read-outs, although analog gauges would eventually prove to be more popular. The interior was roomier, with more cargo space.

Corvette's bid for world-class sports car supremacy was voted *Motor Trend* magazine's 1984 "Car of the Year." The same award was won in 1986 by that year's Corvette convertible, the roadster making its triumphant return after having been absented since 1975. The convertible was the pace car at the running of the 70th Indy 500 race in 1986, and was available in a Corvette special edition replica car.

1986 models offered Bosch anti-lock braking systems as a standard feature. The previous year had seen the installation of gas-pressure shocks, automatically adjusting to maintain a smooth ride over bumpy road conditions; plus, a "Tuned Port" injection engine with an increased 25 horsepower.

In 1987, roller valve lifter helped boost the engine up to 240 horsepower. The car had an in-cockpit tire-pressure monitoring system, a feature it shared with the Porsche 959.

1988 marked Corvette's thirty-fifth anniversary, honored by issuing the car in Polo White, the color of the original 1953 roadster that started it all. The all-white body was subtly accented by thin black strip mid-body trim. The hood emblem was a simple chrome circle bearing the Corvette name. Deep-pocketed enthusiasts could celebrate with the ZO1 anniversary coupes with black-tinted glass roof and fully loaded GT luxury options.

During its midlife, the popular C4 Corvette sold about twenty-five thousand cars yearly, generating sales of roughly 100 million dollars annually. Fuel-efficient engineering to avoid having the car slapped with a government "gas-guzzler" tax was a prime directive at Corvette.

The next challenge would be to maintain those standards while upping the horsepower and supplying eye-opening powerplant punch.

And so the ZR was born.

The eye-catching wheel cover of a 1989 ZR1. An optional Selective Ride Control used gas-pressure shock absorbers to deliver three levels of shock damping for increased readability.

The 1988 Thirty-Fifth Anniversary edition Corvette came in Polo White, the same color as the original 1953 model. Two thousand of these ZO1 coupes with black-tinted glass roofs were produced.

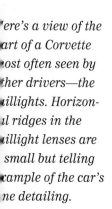

Here's a view of the part of a Corvette most often seen by other drivers—the taillights. Horizontal ridges in the taillight lenses are a small but telling example of the car's fine detailing.

King of the Hill

The 1990 Corvette ZR1 was an engine options package on a subtly modified C4 platform. The car was the fabled "King of the Hill," able to reach 180 miles per hour, rivaling Porsche and Ferrari. The LT5 350-cubic inch V-8 engine had four camshafts and thirty-two valves, high compression, and sequential electronic port fuel injection. The all-aluminum engine was constructed by Mercury Marine, primarily a maker of speedboat and powerboat engines. Topping 375 horsepower, ZR1 could go from zero to sixty in 4.3 seconds.

ZR1's Electronic Throttle Control/ETC used computer chip sensors to "read" the engine's operating condition (temperature, rpms, etc.), monitoring it and adjusting the fuel flow accordingly to obtain optimum performance throughou the ride.

There was an AZF six-speed manual gearbox. The car was unavailable in automatic transmission. A removable hardtop was optional. Inside, there was a new dashboard and six-way seats. A subtle styling detail was the rectangula taillights, instead of the standard round lenses.

The ZR1 cost $627,000, while the standard Corvette coupe cost $37,900. ZR1 owners had to be motivated high-performance fans, but according to them, the car was the best Corvette speed machine since the 1960s. Only two thousand 1990 ZR1s were produced, making this model one of today's prime collectibles.

The 1990 ZR1 was an optional engine package built on a C4 platform, and could go from 0 to 60 mph in 4.3 seconds. Only two thousand were made in 1990, making a hot car even more collectible.

The 1990 ZR1 interior, with a six-speed AZF manual transmission (automatic transmission was unavailable on the model). The six-way adjustable seats have leather seat covers, of course.

The powerplant at the heart of the 1990 ZR1 "King of the Hill," an all-aluminum 350-cid LT5 Mercury Marine 5.7-liter engine, capable of 375-horsepower.

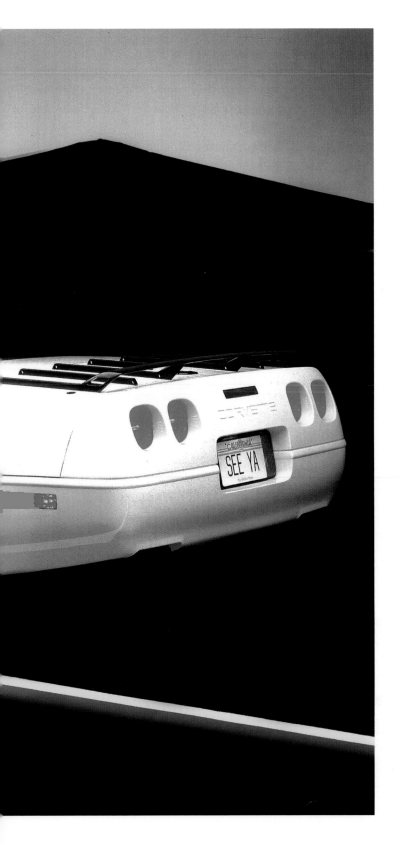

The 1991 Corvette's tail was widened, part of a continuing trend, and the wedge-shaped body had a narrow front end grading to a bulkier tail. The standard engine was a small block L98 350-cubic inch V-8 engine, with 250 horsepower.

1992 saw a new engine debut, as the previous mill was replaced as the standard by the LT1 small block 350-cubic inch V-8 engine with 300 horsepower. The LT1 engine made the regular Corvette almost as fast as the LT5-equipped ZR1, and cost $27,000 less. It put a further ceiling on the ZRl's already low production numbers.

1992 also saw the appointment of Dave Hill as Corvette's Chief engineer, coming in after spending twenty-seven years in Cadillac's engineering department. Russ McLean took the post of Corvette platform manager, while Chuck Jordan continued his tenure as head stylist.

John Schinella, head of the West Coast style studio, made a hit at the 1992 Detroit International Auto Show with his design for Stingray III, a 6-cylinder convertible with a trunk, the first since the trunk space had been swallowed up by the 1963 Sting Ray. The trunk wouldn't make it into the C4, but it would return in the 1997 C5.

There had been talk about a successor to C4 for some time, and the C5 launch had originally been planned for 1993, to coincide with Corvette's fortieth anniversary. The timetable was off and the milestone arrived with no C5 in view.

Stylistically the bodyshell of this 1991 ZR1 is almost identical to the standard C4, but a telltale marker identifying it as a ZR1 is the rectangular taillights. All Corvettes got wider tails that year.

There was a 1993 40th Anniversary Appearance Package Corvette, in coupe and convertible, a C4 with a ruby red paint job and same color leather seats. That year's LT1 engine could go from zero to sixty in 5.4 seconds.

The writing was on the wall for the ZR1, as GM ended production of the LT5 engine at Mercury Marine. Henceforth ZRls would be fitted with LT5s that were already stockpiled, and when the last of them were gone, that would be the last of the ZR1. But it still had a few years left.

Overall, the 1993 Corvette had an improved engine, better suspension, and improved quality construction, eliminating some of the minor rattles and leaks (well, not minor to the owner) caused by the multi-welds of the Bird Cage substructure.

The 1994 Corvette LT1 had sequential port injection and a computerized drivetrain control module. A major event that year was the opening on Labor Day of the National Corvette Museum in Bowling Green, across the street from the assembly plant. The opening event was a weekend Corvette festival as scores of vintage coupes and convertibles gathered at the site, along with some of the creators who had made the car a reality. The museum has been a nonstop success since its doors first opened. That success did not go unnoticed by GM upper management, as it debated whether or not to put C5 into production.

This 1993 C4 coupe benefits from a new standard LT1 350-cid 5.7-liter engine with 300-horsepower, replacing the previous standard L-98 350-cid small block with 250-horsepower. Switchover was made in 1992, in time for Corvette's 40th Anniversary in 1993.

Engineering improvements kept the standard 350-cid overhead V-8 C4 engine enjoying a steady boost in horsepower and fuel efficiency throughout the decade. Corvette engineers hold it as a matter of pride that the mills are never assessed the federal "gas-guzzler" tax penalties.

FOLLOWING PAGE:
The 1994 LT1 was upgraded with sequential port injection, a high-tech computerized drivetrain control module, and a restyled dash. The base price was around $36,000 for a coupe, $44,000 for a convertible.

In 1995, Corvette was honored with its third Indy 500 pace car appearance. The special Collector's Edition Pace Car replica LT1 roadster had an automatic transmission and a set of commemorative decals.

The 1995 Corvette showed some minor style changes, including gills behind the front wheels. For the third time, a Corvette was the pace car at the Indy 500 raceway and, maintaining the tradition, a Pace Car Replica edition was issued. It was an LT1 convertible, purple and white, with automatic transmission and an Indy 500 decal kit.

The 1996 Corvette coupe and convertible had an LT4 5.7-liter V-8 engine option with 330 horsepower. The car had a six-speed manual transmission, four-wheel disc brakes, and aluminum wheels. Optional were run-flat tires, capable of being driven in that condition for 100 miles at 55 miles per hour. There was also a computerized tire pressure monitor system.

On April 2,1995, the last ZR1 was built, and promptly installed in the museum across the street. ZR1 was arguably the best, and definitely the most expensive Corvette of them all. The end of the ZR1 line was marked by a special edition collector's car.

The 1996 model year was the end of the C4 platform. The finishing touch was impending side-impact safety standards. The cost of retooling the assembly process to meet next year's new standards was prohibitive, and became a factor in giving the green light to putting the C5 into production.

New in 1995 were the fender gills behind the front wheels, as seen on this ZR1 coupe. The last ZR1 ever built rolled off the line on April 28,1995, and was promptly installed in Corvette's Bowling Green Museum.

Corvette owners are by definition high performance enthusiasts, but ZR1 owners go even beyond that. They have to, with the ZR1 package adding another $20,000 to the standard price.

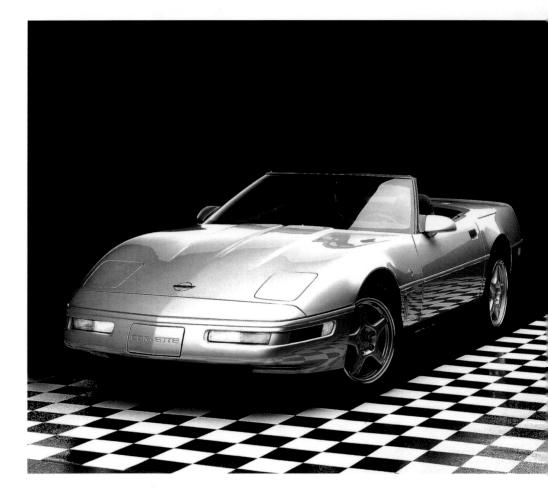

*This 1996 Corvette
Collector Special
Edition roadster
commemorates
the last of the C4s.
By 1996, over 1.1
million Corvettes
had been produced.*

*The 1996 Special
Edition Grand
Sport coupe in
Admiral Blue
and White was
equipped with a
330-horsepower
LT4 engine.
Compare the
styling to the 1956
SR-2 car.*

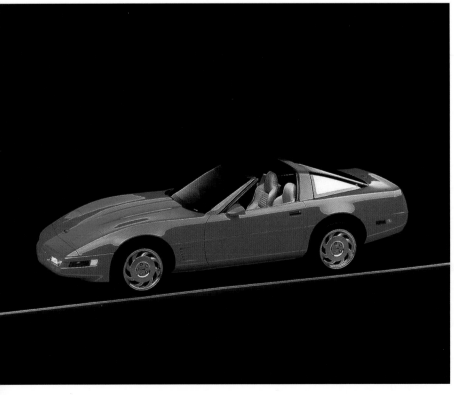

The 1996 Corvette Collector Special Edition roadster. New federal safety standards for beefed-up side-impact protection slated for 1997 would have been too expensive to retool the assembly line, causing the C4 to reach the end of the road.

The 1996 LT4 engine option package's 5.7-liter V-8 could generate 330-horsepower. But the C4 platform would have to make way for its successor tooling up in the wings.

Future Forward

In the early 1990s, Corvette came as close to cancellation as it had been since those shaky early days prior to the 1956 modelsaver. The C4 was popular and respected, the ledger was firmly in the black. What was wrong? The danger lay in the larger corporate environment of GM, whose recent heavy losses, the result of long-term problems, had put the company in serious financial straits. A segment of upper management advocated eliminating Corvette rather than incur the expense of developing the next generation C5. Had this actually happened, it is likely that Corvette could have found the financing to go public and become an independent company, but still: Chevrolet without Corvette? Corvette without Chevy? Unthinkable!

Happily, the short-sighted costcutters were foiled, and the C5 was given the go-ahead. An all-new Corvette was needed for the year 2000 and beyond. Chevy 3 head stylist John Caffaro's design won out, while incorporating the trunk from the Stingray III show car. Breaking with the steel Bird Cage support underpinnings, Chief Engineer Dave Hill came up with the Backbone framework, where a central "tunnel" of shaped steel supports runs through the central axis of the car like a steel spine, stiffening the framework and minimizing vibrations for a smoother ride.

The frame was built according to the revolutionary hydroforming process, where water under ultrahigh pressure was used to shape hollow steel tubes of unprecedented size and length, eliminating countless welded joints and improving overall stability. Another innovation was the composite floor with balsa wood core, which improved stiffness and hence roadability ten times over the previous model.

While C5 was beginning, C4 was ending. The last C4 rolled off the line on June 21,1996, and was bought by an Illinois collector for his private museum.

In its wake came the 1997 Corvette C5 coupe, built to compete against the Nissan 300ZX, Toyota Supra, Dodge Viper, Porsche 911 Carrera, and the few others in that high-powered breed.

The C5 has an all-aluminum LS1 347-cubic inch pushrod V-8 engine with sequential multi-port injection and 345 horsepower. That makes the C5 second only to ZR1 in speed, capable of going from zero to sixty in 4.7 seconds and topping out at 172 miles per hour.

C5's hood and fender assembly are similar to the C4 platform. The aero roof has a bubble effect, while lower corner front scoops magnify the machine's aggressive frontality. The four oval repeater lamps have no wraparound. Big rear depth is accented by oversized Goodyear rear tires with flat spoke wheels.

Under the skin, hydroformed stiff frame rails, the longest in any automobile made, provide vibration-dampening stability. There's Magnateer II rack-and-pinion steering and a dual exhaust system. A rear upper arm suspension system provides added driving control. There's a removable hardtop, too.

The car has a six-speed Borg Warner manual transmission, with special clutch and brake alloy pedals. Electronic Throttle Control is standard on C5. The dashboard is equipped with analog instrument gauges, while the Driver Information Center/DIC console screen has digital readouts. Coming soon is a heads-up visual display system, similar to those used in fighter planes, where the instrument display is light-projected so it appears to be floating in the lower part of the windshield, above the hood.

C5 has won industry-wide raves and intense popular interest, which only increased with the arrival of the promised 1998 C5 convertible.

As Corvette approached the half-century mark, the future looked bright. In the words of the motto of the C5 production team, *"The legend lives."*

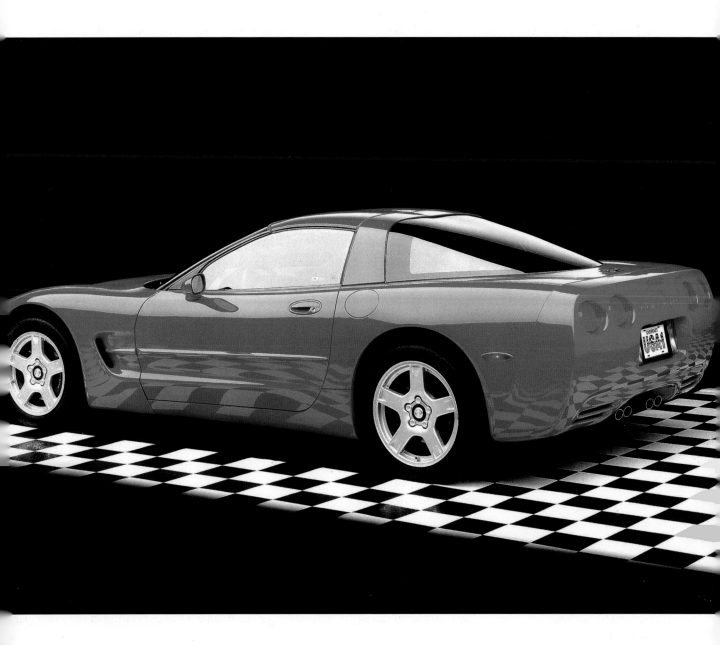

The 1997 C5 bodyshell features an aero-styled bubble roof and big
rear depth, including the first trunk on a Corvette since 1962. The
rear upper arm suspension system gives added control on the road,
where a C5 can go from 0 to 60 in 4.7 seconds. Catch it if you can!

CHAPTER FOUR

THE 21ST-CENTURY CORVETTE

The fifth generation of the Corvette, produced from 1997 through 2004, ushered in a bold, exciting new era in the history of America's sports car. Bumper to bumper, the much-anticipated C5 'Vette marked a radical departure from the C4 series. This latest one introduced a wind-tunnel-tested outer shell, a totally redesigned frame that improved the car's ride and handling, and the 345-hp, LS1 V-8, Chevrolet's first all-aluminum, small-block engine. "The C5 is a refined Corvette in all the right ways," boasted Dave Hill, the car's new chief engineer at the time.

The 1997 model was only offered as a hatchback coupe. Its wider, ergonomic design made getting in and out easier, provided greater visibility, and overall was more comfortable and functional to drive. Unlike previous models that bolted the transmission right behind the engine, this one's was relocated back between the rear wheels. The frame featured hydroformed side frame rails, each made from a single piece of tubular steel, for added strength. "In its 45-year history," gushed Motor Trend, "the Corvette has never before been so excellent in so many ways relative to its competition. It's a colossal achievement."

A convertible C5 model was reintroduced in 1998, and for the first time since 1962, this ragtop included a trunk accessed from outside the car. Buyers could not only opt for a lighter version with magnesium wheels, but also a blueish-purple replica of the Corvette pace car from that year's Indianapolis 500.

Chevy closed out the 20th century by offering three different models of the 1999 'Vette: a convertible; a hatchback coupe; and a fixed-roof coupe, available only with a six-speed manual transmission. In a *Car & Driver* road test, the hardtop turned the quarter-mile in 13.2 seconds at 110 mph.

Welcome to the New Millennium

The C5 series was turning heads and generating brisk sales by 2000, yet the first Corvette of the 21st century arrived with relatively little fanfare. Most apparent was the absence of the passenger-side door lock cylinder, deemed redundant with the keyless entry system, and the addition of five-spoke, forged-aluminum wheels. Otherwise, two new exterior colors were available—Millennium Yellow and Dark Bowling Green Metallic—along with a novel Torch Red interior.

The Corvette embarked on a space-age odyssey in 2001 with the introduction of the limited-edition Z06 fixed-roof coupe. The name was borrowed from the race-ready Sting Rays built in 1963. This high-tech Z06 was, in Chevy's words, "aimed directly at diehard performance enthusiasts at the upper end of the high-performance market." Ample evidence was revealed under the hood, where the LS1 engine was replaced by a more powerful 385-hp LS6 V-8, capable of launching the Z06 at a blazing speed of 170 mph. A stiffer suspension, lightweight wheels, and wider Goodyear tires added to its utter drivability. The 2002 Z06 packed an even greater wallop when the LS6 was boosted to 405-hp.

Corvette fans were thrilled with the look of the 2001 Z06, but it was what under the hood that really thrilled them: a 385-hp V-8.

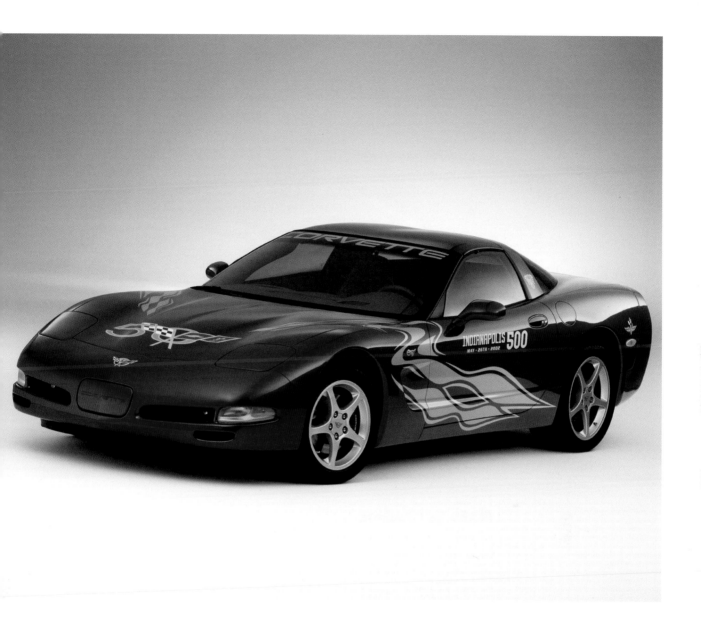

For the 2003 model year, the Corvette's keepers at Chevrolet hailed the marque's first five glorious decades with a special 50th anniversary edition. "As we celebrate our golden anniversary," said Corvette brand manager Rick Baldick, "we honor our past and cast a bright eye toward the future." That was manifested in a special model, available as either a coupe or convertible, dressed up with a shiny burgundy paint job, a dark gray-colored interior, champagne-colored aluminum wheels, and 50th Anniversary emblems—still relatively affordable even after paying an extra $5,000.

The C5 period closed out in 2004 with commemorative editions of all three models. They featured a painted carbon-fiber hood, a first for a production vehicle in North America, and an improved shock system. To laud Corvette's racing glory, a special LeMans edition was available, and a 'Vette once again paced the Indy 500.

To honor the Corvette's 50th anniversary, this 'Vette was used as the pace car at the Indianapolis 500, perhaps the world's most famous auto race.

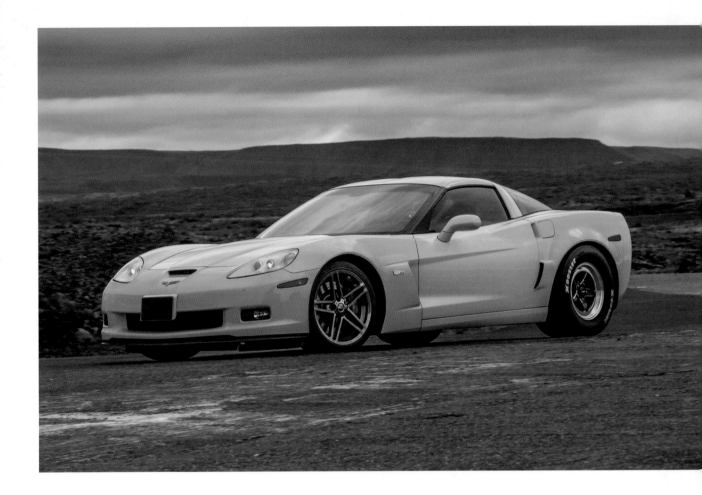

Sixth Sensation

The long-awaited sixth-generation Corvette finally debuted in January 2005. The newly designed and engineered C6—the fastest, most powerful car ever produced by Chevy and all of General Motors—boasted a long list of improvements on the already-spectacular C5. Chevy didn't tinker with the front engine and rear transmission setup, but did create a tidier, lighter, 5.1-inch-shorter package on a longer wheelbase. The C6's softly rounded contours made its shell the most aerodynamic to date, and exposed headlights returned for the first time since 1962. Under the hood roared a new 6.0-liter LS2 V-8 engine, which pumped out 400 hp and 400 lb-ft of torque. In Edmunds.com's initial road test, a '05 coupe outfitted with the standard six-speed manual transmission reached 60 mph in 4.8 seconds and blitzed the quarter-mile in 12.9 seconds at 109.1 mph. Already the most-affordable high-performance sports car in the world, the C6 base price was $290 lower than its predecessor's.

A redesigned Z06 was unleashed in 2006 after a one-year absence from the lineup. The frame of the Z06 incorporated lighter-but-stronger aluminum vs. steel components, while the shell's rear end sported wide-body fenders and a stabilizing spoiler. Up front, carbon-fiber fenders replaced weightier fiberglass, and they were flared to accommodate larger wheels, tires, and brakes. The standard C6 coupe and convertible Corvettes were zippy enough with their 400-hp LS2 V-8s, but the Z06 one-upped them with its power-packed new LS7 small-block V-8 that kicked out 505 hp. "In many ways, the LS7 is a racing engine in a street car," remarked Dave Muscaro, assistant chief engineer of the Corvette's V-8s.

After blowing the doors off the competition with the 2005 C6 (left), the company kept the motor running with the debut of the 2006 Z06 with improved engine power and refined body styling.

The 2007 'Vette added a little more pep to its LS7 step, sprinting the quarter-mile in 12.0 seconds flat at 121.8 mph. That apparently wasn't enough for the engineers, though, so in 2008 they broke out a new base engine—a 6.2-liter LS3 version of the small-block V-8, rated at 430 hp. In the cockpit, a leather-wrap interior was optional, and outside, the wheels flashed a new five-spoke design.

Harking back to 1993 and the Corvette's 40th anniversary, Chevy unveiled the ZR1 for 2009. It was powered by the new supercharged LS9 engine, a 6.2-liter V-8 beast that pumped out 638 hp—four times the original Corvette's engine's—and a top speed of 205 mph. Other ZR1 highlights included multiple carbon-fiber aerodynamic upgrades and massive carbon-ceramic brakes.

Corvette ushered in the second decade of the new millennium by bringing back the Grand Sport name to the brand's illustrious lineup. This entirely new model series, available as either a coupe or convertible, replaced the Z51 performance package option, making it basically an LS3-equipped Z06 with a steel frame instead of aluminum. This latest C6 featured wider bodywork and tires, plus a dry-sump oiling system on manual-transmission models. With increased safety always top of mind, side airbags became standard on all models.

At an incredible 638 HP, the 2009 Corvette ZR1 boasted one of the most powerful engines ever put in a Corvette model.

For 2011, the Corvette was offered in seven different models—the most in the marque's history—including the Z06 Carbon Limited Edition in celebration of the 50th anniversary of the 'Vette first competing at the 24 Hours of Le Mans, in 1960. This special Z06 had a 7.0-liter, 505-hp V-8 under the hood, the ZR1's 15-inch carbon-ceramic brakes, driver-adjustable "smart fluid" shocks, black 19-inch front and 20-inch rear wheels, and Michelin Pilot PS2 tires. Exactly 500 Z06 Carbon models were produced, with exteriors available only in Supersonic Blue or Inferno Orange.

Another special 'Vette was rolled out in 2012, this one in honor of the 100th anniversary of Chevrolet. The Centennial Edition package—available for all models—included Carbon Flash Metallic paint, satin-black graphics, satin-black wheels with a red stripe, an assortment of Centennial badges, an Ebony leather interior with suede accents, and Magnetic Selective Ride Control. Following a year away from the Brickyard track, the Corvette returned to pace the Indy 500, with celebrity chef Guy Fieri behind the wheel.

The Corvette turned 60 in 2013, which also marked the grand finale of the C6 series. To celebrate the birthday, Chevy offered a 60th Anniversary package including Arctic White exterior paint, a special Blue Diamond interior, optional blue exterior stripes, and carbon trim. Separately, a one-year-only 427 Convertible was released. An LS7-powered drop-top, based on the Grand Sport model, it featured a six-speed manual transmission, carbon hood, and Z06 front carbon fenders.

In classic black, this limited-edition 2012 Corvette honored Chevy's 100th anniversary, and also led the way at the Indy 500.

Seventh Heaven

It's safe to say that the Corvette stylists and engineers are constantly working to improve upon America's beloved sports car. They started imagining its seventh incarnation back in 2007, delayed the rollout for three years, then finally introduced the all-new C7 series for 2014 model year. While aiming for the millennial audience, Corvette brought back their fathers' Stingray name—though it was hardly pop's car. A hardtop version, with a carbon-fiber roof and hood, debuted at the Detroit Auto Show in January 2013; two months later, the Stingray convertible was unveiled at the Geneva Auto Show. Both were powered by a new LT1 engine, a 6.2-liter version of the GM small-block V-8, rated at 455 hp, making it the Corvette's most powerful base engine ever. Constructed around an all-aluminum frame, the standard model featured a new seven-speed manual transmission, while a six-speed automatic was optional.

For the 2015 model year, Chevrolet announced the return of the Z06, powered by a LT4 6.2-liter aluminum V-8 engine with 650 hp. Deemed as the most race-

The amazing Stingray made a big return, as Chevy brought back the famous name with two different looks—a hardtop (left) and a sleek convertible.

Fast spin in a 'Vette

Picture yourself in this driver's seat of the awesome 2016 Corvette Z06, ready to put the pedal to the metal and take this amazing car (right) through its paces. Start your engines!

eady 'Vette yet, the Z06 was also the first to offer a supercharged engine, automatic transmission, and convertible option. After its first road test, Car & Driver declared that "the Z06 must be ranked among the world's best."

The 2016 Corvette Z06 C7.R Edition paid homage to the brand's illustrious racing legacy. It was offered in Corvette Racing's signature yellow livery, or n black, with coordinated exterior and interior accents. Only 500 examples vere built, in either coupe or convertible models, and all included the Z07 performance package, with carbon ceramic brakes and Michelin PS Cup 2 tires, nd the LT4 engine.

The Corvette Grand Sport was back for 2017, recalling the racing spirit of the riginal 1963 GS model. The new version featured a 6.2-liter LT1 V-8 engine, apable of 460 hp and 465 lb.-ft. of torque, and a compact design that lowered he hoodline and maximized aerodynamics. Even as Corvette collectors and nthusiasts were ogling this latest supercar, rumors abounded that the C8 eries was imminent, possibly featuring a long-fabled mid-engine model.

RESEARCH PROJECTS

1. The TV show Route 66 (CBS, 1960-64) "starred" a Corvette driven by two young dudes driving around the country. While not specifically about Rte. 66, that is a famous American road. What different Vettes did the drive during the series' run? What are some of the landmarks across Rte. 66? What late singer recorded a hit song by the same name in 1946?

2. Why was the Corvette chosen as the official pace car of the Indianapolis 500 in 1978? And how many times has it fulfilled that honor since then, and what models were featured?

3. Find some other movies or TV shows that featured the Corvette or the Stingray. Write a review of one of them based on how much the car played a part in the movie or show!

4. The Corvette has undergone several facelifts over the years. Get out your drawing pad and create your own new "look" for the 'Vette. What would you change or add? How would you modify it to make it truly yours but still retain classic Corvette styling?

FIND OUT MORE

Books

Edsall, Larry. *Corvette Stingray: The Seventh Generation of America's Sports Car*. Minneapolis: Motorbooks, 2014.

Ludvigsen, Karl. *Corvette: America's Star-Spangled Sports Car: 1953–1982*. Cambridge, MA: Bentley Publishers, 2014.

Mueller, Mike. *The Complete Book of Corvette — Revised & Updated: Every Model Since 1953*. Minneapolis: Motorbooks, 2014.

Web Sites

www.chevrolet.com/corvette-sports-cars.html

www.blog.caranddriver.com/chevrolet-corvette-timeline-milestones-and-more-from-c1-through-c7

www.corvettemuseum.org

www.nationalcorvetteowners.com

SERIES GLOSSARY OF KEY TERMS

aerodynamics the study of how air moves over and around an object

camshaft the metal rod to which pistons are attached in a car engine

chassis the metal internal framework or skeleton of a car

coupe generally used as a term for a two-door car

endurance a type of racing that is conducted over a long time period

ergonomic designed to mold or fit a person's body shape

fuel injection a process in some car engines that sends a small amount of fuel into each of the engine's many tiny combustions

grille automotive term for the front end of a car

horsepower a measurement of engine strength, based on the power that a single horse could achieve

marque a name for an automaker's logos or car models

rpm revolutions per minute, the number of times the camshaft spins in that time period

sedan typically, a four-door car

suspension the series of springs and bars that support a car while it drives

tachometer a device that measures rpms in an engine

turbocharged describing a car engine that has additional parts that drive more air into the combustion chambers, thus increasing power of the car

transmission the set of gears that transfers power from the engine to the wheels of a car; in a manual transmission, the drivers moves a lever that makes the gears change; in automatic transmission, the car moves from gear to gear itself.

INDEX

INDEX

PHOTO CREDITS

All photographs 1-79 by Ron Kimball, Mountain View, California, with the exception of the following: National Motor Museum: 7, 26 (bottom), 29 (bottom), 34 (top), 39, 47, 58 (top); Nicky Wright/National Motor Museum: 3–4, 20, 21 (top), 22, 23 (bottom), 29 (top), 37, 43, 45, 46 (bottom), 49, 53, 54, 58 (botom), 59, 65 (top), 66, 67 (top); Dreamstime. com: Piotr Wawrzyniuk 80, Johan68 84, Steirus 85, Valley Snow 86, Darren Brodie 87, Tomstox 88; Chevrolet Media Images: 89–91.